THE SALEM WITCH TRIALS

A PRIMARY SOURCE HISTORY OF THE WITCHCRAFT TRIALS IN SALEM, MASSACHUSETTS

JENNY MACBAIN

rosen central

Primary Source

For my grandmother, Helen Weiss

Published in 2003 by The Rosen Publishing Group, Inc.
29 East 21st Street, New York, NY 10010

Library of Congress Cataloging-in-Publication Data

MacBain, Jenny.
The Salem witch trials : a primary source history of the witchcraft trials in Salem, Massachusetts / by Jenny MacBain.– 1st ed.
   p. cm. — (Primary sources in American history)
Summary: Uses primary source documents, narrative, and illustrations to recount the history of the witch hunt and trials that occurred in Salem, Massachusetts, in the seventeenth century.
Includes bibliographical references and index.
ISBN 0-8239-3683-X
1. Trials (Witchcraft)—Massachusetts—Salem—Juvenile literature.
2. Witchcraft—Massachusetts—Salem—History—Juvenile literature. [1. Trials (Witchcraft)—Massachusetts—Salem. 2. Witchcraft—Massachusetts—Salem.
3. Salem (Mass.)—History—Colonial period, ca. 1600–1775.] I. Title. II. Series.
KF2478.8.W5 M33 2002
133.4'3'097445—dc21

                                        2002000673

Manufactured in the United States of America

CONTENTS

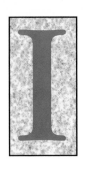NTRODUCTION

When the Puritans set up their small community in Massachusetts in 1630, they had no idea what horrible events would occur decades later. After the Pilgrims fled religious persecution and came to America in 1620, 20,000 immigrants established colonies in America in a period of just twelve years. These colonists were mostly English, with a mix of German, Swedish, Dutch, and French.

ALONE IN THE WILDERNESS

Whereas the Pilgrims wanted to separate completely from the religious laws of the Church of England, the Puritans wanted to reform, or purify, these doctrines. The Puritans, many of whom settled in Salem, Massachusetts, believed that every human being was predestined to enter either heaven or hell.

In 1620, the Pilgrims settled in Plymouth, about fifty miles south of what became Salem, where wealthy Puritan merchants created the Massachusetts Bay Colony. Ten years later, the Puritans set up their own government and laws, as had the Pilgrims.

In 1672, the governing body of Massachusetts, the General Court, gave the men of Salem Village—the farming section of

Salem—permission to lay plans for a meetinghouse. In 1689, Reverend Samuel Parris was elected as minister. By examining various documents, historians have discovered that Parris was an extremely stern man who was obsessed with the idea of sin and his own self-importance. His wife, Elizabeth, was very sickly and was often confined to her bed. Because Parris was often away on church business, his family was frequently left alone.

By 1692, the area of Salem—which consisted of the prosperous Salem Town and Salem Village—had over 600 residents. There was tension between the town and the farming village. The agricultural community wanted to govern themselves instead of having to rely on the financial support of the town. The farmers felt that the town was becoming too modern and that Puritan values were not being upheld.

In February 1692, Parris's nine-year-old daughter, Betty, and her eleven-year-old cousin, Abigail Williams (who had been orphaned and lived at the Parris home), began exhibiting strange behavior. When Parris returned home from work one day, he found the girls contorting themselves in impossible positions, cowering under chairs, sticking out their tongues, and screaming gibberish. Lacking any natural explanation, Parris's physician, Dr. William Griggs, decided that the girls were "bewitched."

In the seventeenth century, under British law, colonists found to have been consorting with witches or the devil were guilty of having committed a felony. This felony was punishable by hanging. On February 29, 1692, the first arrest warrants were issued for three women whom the girls claimed had afflicted them. About two hundred more arrests were made in the coming months by different people. In May, pressured into putting an end to the madness, Governor William Phipps set up the Special Court of Oyer and Terminer (to "hear and determine"), which was finally dissolved in October when the trials came to an end.

People have been wondering for over three hundred years why the Salem witch trials happened. Some researchers think that ergot, a fungus that replaces kernels in rye, affected people's mental state and increased paranoia when they ingested it unknowingly. However, it's also possible that those who accused others of witchcraft were hallucinating. Other

A Theory

Historian Carol F. Karlsen writes in *The Devil in the Shape of a Woman: Witchcraft in Colonial England*, "Many of the accused were women with property . . . [No] male heirs constituted a threat to an economic system based on the orderly transfer of property from father to son." In some cases, if these wealthy women were imprisoned, the state, or government, could steal their land. Several of the accused women had been married more than once; others were wealthy and well-established widows. In Puritan New England, it was considered the work of the devil to be too "willful." If women were alone, this revealed a certain "high handedness."

historians argue that the conflicts grew out of the rising merchant class in Salem Town. Possibly, the merchants stepped on the toes of the agricultural community to achieve more wealth and power, and the farmers retaliated. Several researchers believe the accusations were fueled by one family: the Putnams.

Historian Richard Trask believes that the witch trials were nothing but a case of "clinical hysteria." Whatever the reason, Salem—its residents uprooted from their mother country and isolated in the woods—was about to face a devastating year.

TIMELINE

1609 —— Henry Hudson leads explorations in Massachusetts Bay.

1620 —— Pilgrims arrive in America on the *Mayflower* and establish Plymouth.

1626 —— The Naumkeag Indians occupy various sites in Massachusetts. Roger Conant establishes Salem as a trading post.

1629 —— Merchants, who simply want to reform, or "purify," the Calvinist Church, establish the Massachusetts Bay Colony. A royal charter gives them a right to govern lands in what is present-day Massachusetts. John Endecott begins the first plantation in Salem.

1630 —— John Winthrop is appointed the new governor and sails to Massachusetts.

1638 —— A small group of Puritans settle in what becomes known as Salem Village.

1649 —— In England, Charles I is executed.

1672 —— Salem Village acquires authority to begin a parish, hire a minister, and gather taxes for community improvements.

TIMELINE

1689 —— Salem Village Church is formed, and Samuel Parris becomes minister.

January 1692 – Girls in Salem Village begin to exhibit strange physical "fits," and William Griggs concludes they are "bewitched." The girls are pressured to identify who is afflicting them.

February 1692 – Magistrates Johnathan Hathorne and Jonathan Corwin "examine" several of the accused.

May 1692 —— Governor William Phipps sets up the Special Court of Oyer and Terminer "to hear and determine" the witchcraft cases.

June 1692 —— Bridget Bishop is the first person to be found guilty of witchcraft and is hanged.

October 29, 1692 —— Governor Phipps terminates the Court of Oyer and Terminer.

1752 —— Salem Village changes its name to Danvers and is established as a separate district.

CHAPTER 1

PLANTING THE SEEDS

In 1692, Salem Village consisted mostly of what is now Danvers, Massachusetts, as well as most of present-day Middletown and Peabody. Things were difficult for the inhabitants of Salem Village at that time. In addition to the severe climate, there was always the threat of smallpox epidemics, Indian attacks, land wars, and political upheaval from England to contend with. During this time, Salem Town was becoming a major trading post and many immigrants were coming to the area. These newcomers were a threat to the conservative Puritans. Puritans were taught to be pious and serene as adults, and children were expected to behave like small adults. Play was not allowed. In fact, it was viewed as a form of laziness. Perhaps as a way to escape this rigid lifestyle, nine-year-old Betty Parris and eleven-year-old Abigail Williams—who were often joined

In 1866, W. P. Upham created this map of Salem as the town was in 1692. The area was marshy, and the winters were harsh. In 1692, the population of the village was approximately 600. These inhabitants lived in ninety houses that were scattered over an area measuring twenty square miles. This map is housed at the Danvers Alarm List Company, Inc., in Massachusetts (an alarm was a group of soldiers). The Danvers Alarm List Company, Inc., is a re-created eighteenth-century militia unit. It portrays historically accurate militia, alarm companies, and colonial life in what today is known as Danvers (formerly Salem Village).

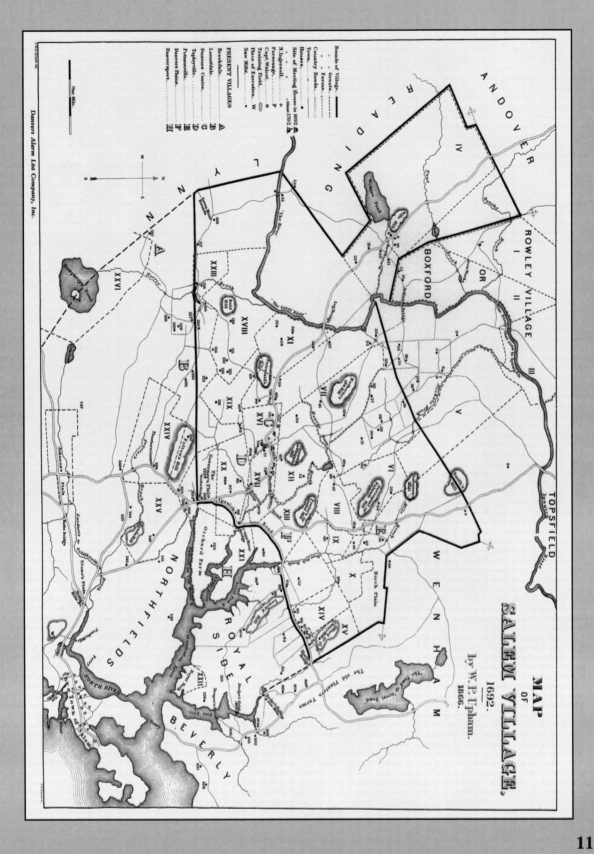

MAP
OF
SALEM VILLAGE,
1692.
by W.P. Upham.
1866.

11

by a small group of girls—played fortune-telling games in secret. In one game, the girls would ask questions about the future and then drop an egg white into a glass of water to see what shape it took. One February night in 1692, Betty Parris saw a picture of a coffin, and suddenly her body began to contort into odd shapes and she started screaming. How could they find out who was torturing her? One of Parris's servants, John Indian, baked a "witch cake" made of rye meal and the girls' urine. John Indian would then feed this cake to the Parris's dog, and if he acted strangely, the adults could determine whether or not the girls were indeed bewitched.

Who were the accused? The first women accused of witch-craft, Tituba (who was in her twenties), thirty-nine-year-old Sarah Good, and forty-nine-year-old Sarah Osbourne, lived in what is now known as Danvers Central. Sarah Good was a beggar woman. Sarah Osbourne had a questionable past: She had married her Irish manservant, Alexander Osbourne, and wasn't considered very smart.

The accused were first "examined" by Judges Johnathan Hathorne and Jonathan Corwin at the Salem Village meeting-house. The "examinations" consisted of harsh questioning. According to Frances Hill in *A Delusion of Satan*, a judge would bully and scream at an accused person, asking, "What familiarity have you with the devil?" The person being questioned would be terrified. Then there would be invasive probing to discover a "witch's mark." A mark could be anything from a pinprick to a freckle to a birthmark. These searches were, at best, humiliating.

Shortly after Abigail Williams and Betty Parris accused these women, twelve-year-old Ann Putnam Jr., seventeen-year-old Mary Walcott, and seventeen-year-old Elizabeth Hubbard (the niece of Dr. William Griggs, who had labeled Abigail and Betty "bewitched") also began to exhibit "fits," and they, too, accused a slew of people. It is possible that Ann, who lived only a mile away at farmer Thomas Putnam's house, or Mary Walcott, who lived only a few hundred yards from Betty and Abigail, also joined in on the fortune-telling games.

According to some accounts, these girls formed a spiritual circle, or a coven, to try to foretell their futures. Young Ann became a sort of ringleader of the group, accusing the most people of witchcraft. It is possible that these girls half believed that they really were being "afflicted" by witches.

Perhaps Sarah Good and Sarah Osbourne were targeted as witches because they had bad reputations in the community. Tituba was the girls' caregiver and was constantly in their presence. For other accused persons, it might have been personal politics that sent them to their deaths. Some historians believe that Ann Putnam Jr. was acting on the behalf of her parents, Thomas and Ann Sr., who had many motives (as we will see later on) for wanting to get rid of certain individuals.

No matter what her motives were, Ann Putnam Jr. was responsible for the imprisonment and eventual hanging of many innocent people.

To understand the grave situation in Salem in 1692, one must examine the life of Betty Parris's father, Reverend Samuel Parris. Reverend Parris lived in the Salem Village parsonage after the departure of Reverend George Burroughs, who was later accused of witchcraft. Parris's father, Thomas Parris, had an estate in Barbados, and when Thomas passed away, the younger Parris went there to settle the affairs of the sugar plantation. When Parris left the island in 1680, he took two slaves with him: Tituba and John Indian. He moved to Boston and soon married Elizabeth Eldridge.

This photo comes from the Danvers Preservation Commission. This large, white, colonial home is the Samuel Holten house, built in 1670. Sarah Holten, who gave damaging testimony against Rebecca Nurse, lived here. Sarah testified in court that Rebecca told her son Benjamin to go and get a gun and kill all of the pigs on the Holten farm. Then Sarah blamed Rebecca for her husband's death. According to documents from the Massachusetts Historical Society, Sarah Holten stated, "My poor husband . . . he was taken with a strange fit and struck blind."

In 1686, Parris began substituting for absent ministers, and he campaigned to be the new Salem Village preacher.

The Putnam family handpicked Parris to be their new minister. The influential Putnams owned the most farmland in Salem Village, and they used their wealth to establish their own church congregation. They opposed the modern ways of Salem Town and wanted to separate from it. Over half of the village congregation were Putnams. The Putnams paid Parris a small salary and provided him with firewood. He also received money from local taxes. But Reverend Parris also got several extra bonuses from the Putnam family.

Parris was also able to obtain the title and deed to the parsonage and the surrounding land. This newfound ownership gave him stability and power. This was a rare transaction for the time period.

In October 1691, a new Salem Village committee was assembled. The committee, mostly opponents of Parris from

This photo is of the Rebecca Nurse Homestead (built in the early seventeenth century), which is located at 149 Pine Street. This house is a perfect example of a colonial farmstead with a family burial plot on the grounds. Nurse's unmarked grave is located on this plot. On the grounds there is a monument to Rebecca Nurse. The Salem community was shocked when Nurse was charged with witchcraft and brought before a grand jury. Her trial prompted normally fearful people to come forward and speak out against the injustice.

Salem Village, refused to pay the local tax. They also questioned his ownership of the ministry house. He feared he would lose his position. Parris made sermons about how evil was taking over Salem Village and how there were conspiracies by the devil at work. With Parris losing money (taxes paid his salary), the Putnams feared they would lose him and the formation of a new community that the congregation brought.

When Betty Parris and Abigail Williams had fits, Parris called on his powerful friends to hold prayer meetings and days of fasting, hoping these things would rid the girls of evil. He supposedly beat his servant Tituba into confessing. Tituba's life was spared only because she had confessed out of terror.

What happened to the other women who were accused? Sarah Good stayed in jail for months and was finally sentenced on June 29, 1692. She was hanged on July 19. Sarah Osbourne would never set foot outside prison walls again; she died in prison on May 10, 1692. Throughout 1692, hundreds of people were

This is an engraving of Judge William Stoughton by R. Babson, circa 1780. William Stoughton lived from 1631 to 1701. He was appointed the chief magistrate over the Court of Oyer and Terminer (the special court that heard the witch trials). Though well educated, having received a degree in theology from Harvard and an M.A. from Oxford, he lacked any legal education or training. Under Stoughton, procedures in the courtroom deviated from the norm: He tolerated private discussions between the judges and the accusers, and he forbade any defense for the accused. Despite his role in perpetuating the trials, Stoughton suffered little political damage after the hysteria died down.

accused of witchcraft. The magistrates of the Massachusetts Bay Colony began preparations to question the accused.

The private questioning and examinations in quiet rooms gave way to public courtroom dramas. At these trials, over forty people confessed to being witches. In some cases, those confessing accused others. It is not surprising that people were not emotionally or intellectually equipped to defend themselves against the bullying judges. Ironically, those who confessed were often let go, and those who proclaimed they were innocent Christians ended up going to jail or being hanged.

When the governor of Salem, Sir William Phipps, set foot on Massachusetts soil with his minister friend and president of

Harvard, Increase Mather, in mid-May 1692, accusations of sorcery were flying, examinations were under way, and people were already awaiting further trials. This was an important visit, however, because Mather brought with him the colony's new charter. The previous charter proclaimed that instead of being a self-governing body, the colony had to be ruled by a governor from England. But that charter had expired at the end of 1689 when English king James II was overthrown. The colony had been without a valid government for two years. It was during this time that witchcraft mania began. Before any laws from this new charter could be put into effect, Phipps watched as hysteria grew in Salem. He felt that he had to take action.

As recorded in *A Delusion of Satan*, Phipps wrote in his diary: "When I first arrived I found this province [most] miserably harassed with a most horrible witchcraft or possession of devils."

As an emergency measure, Phipps set up the Court of Oyer and Terminer. William Stoughton, a friend of William Phipps's, was very excited to take his new post: chief magistrate. Born in 1631, Stoughton possessed an ongoing interest in government. Stoughton is remembered for his role in the trials as being one of the most relentless judges of his time. Historians tend to discuss him at length because he admitted spectral evidence into the courtroom, which was very effective in prosecuting people. Puritans believed that witches could send out their specters, or spirits, from the inside of their bodies. These specters had human powers of sight, hearing, and touch, and could transport themselves out of prison cells or fly through the air at will.

After the prestigious Special Court of Oyer and Terminer (made up of seven judges) was established, it was not long

The first woman to be hanged in Salem was Bridget Bishop. This is a sketch of Bishop's hanging by an unknown artist, date unknown. Bishop was the first accused witch sentenced for execution by the Court of Oyer and Terminer. On occasion, Bishop wore a bodice with the color red woven through it. This manner of dress was considered inappropriate by the community. In addition to having been married three times, Bishop also ran a tavern at her house and she was accused of drinking apple cider all night. Also, she was previously accused of witchcraft years earlier and was known for quarreling with her husband in public, which was against the law. Ten years earlier, Bishop had been forced to stand back-to-back, bound and gagged in the center of town with her husband, Thomas Oliver, because they had quarreled in public. When Bishop was accused of witchcraft, there was no one to come to her defense: Bishop didn't have any powerful friends.

before someone suffered from its judgment. On June 10, 1692, Bridget Bishop (fifty-two years old) became the first witch to be hanged on Gallows Hill. Though the afflicted girls had never formerly met Bishop, they knew her by reputation. Bishop had been taken to court twelve years earlier on a witchcraft charge. Though she had been found innocent, there remained rumors of her activities.

At the trial on June 2, 1692, fifty-year-old Deliverance Hobbs, who had been watching the trials, stated that Bishop had wanted her to "sign the Devil's book or she would whip her with iron rods." Other townspeople came forward with more testimony. Samuel Gray claimed that fourteen years earlier, Bishop had killed his child. Later, when Gray was on his deathbed, he confessed that this was a lie. At eight o'clock in the morning, Bishop was carried on a cart from the Salem jail, along Prison Lane, to Essex Street, out of town to Boston Road, and then to a steep, rocky hill to be hanged from a tree.

CHAPTER 2

EXAMINATIONS, PINPRICKS, AND PRISONS

Considering that Rebecca Nurse had recently been ill, historians have stated that the seventy-one-year-old woman was probably pulled out of bed when she was arrested on March 23, 1692. Even though Nurse claimed that she was innocent, she was still "examined" by Judges Hathorne and Corwin. Nurse also had to endure two physical examinations from midwives. Sometimes, midwives would provide contradictory statements and the accused would have to be looked at a third time. Citizens who made complaints against supposed witches were then brought before the magistrates for preliminary hearings. When the magistrates felt that there was

There are only segments remaining of the original "Examination of Rebecca Nurse." Parts of it have been torn over time. The original document is at the Peabody Essex Museum in Salem, Massachusetts. The handwriting on the examination is that of Reverend Samuel Parris. Typically, when accused witches were being "examined," they were kept in jail at night and brought to the meetinghouse for questioning during the day, either together or separately. There was much drama involved in the procedure of the examinations. The magistrates rode on horseback from the town in a formal procession, accompanied by marshals carrying spears. Once inside, the accusers gave testimony on what the "witch" had done to them. See page 53 for a transcript of the document.

The Examination
of Rebecka Nurse at Salem Village
24. Mar. 1691/2

Mr. Hathorn - What do you say (speaking to one afflicted) Hath
you seen this woman hurt you?
Yes, she beat me this morning
Abigail Have you been hurt by this Woman?
Yes
Ann Putnam in a grievous fit cryed out that
she hurt her.
Goody Nurse, here are two An: Putnam the child &
Abigail Williams complains of your hurting them
what do you say to it
N. I can say before my Eternal father I am innocent, &
God will clear my innocency

— — —

you do know whither you are guilty, & have familiarity
with the Devil, & now when you are here present to
see such a thing as these testify a black man whis-
pering in your ear, & birds about you what do you
say to it
It is all false I am clear

— — —

Is it not an unaccountable case that when they
you are examined these persons are afflicted
& have got no body to look to but God

John Hathorne
Janathan Corwin ⨍

FRAGMENT OF EXAMINATION OF REBECCA NURSE,
In Handwriting of Rev. Samuel Parris.[1]

enough evidence for a trial, the accused was put in jail and had to wait for a hearing before a grand jury.

At the time, people felt that if the witches were chained up, they had less chance of releasing their specters out to attack people. Often, they were placed in ankle-to-neck chains. When the witches were locked up, the town waited to see if the girls' fits would cease. They, of course, did not. This brought on other arrests and examinations. While Nurse was being examined, middle-aged community member Elizabeth Proctor was denounced as a witch on March 28, and Nurse's sister, Sarah Cloyce, was accused on April 3. John Proctor, sixty, was also accused and imprisoned.

Rebecca Nurse was the perfect image of Puritan piety. If some-one like her could be accused of witchcraft, then no one in Salem was safe. Rebecca Nurse, born in 1621, was the daughter of William Towne and Joanna Blessing. She had two sisters, Mary Easty, fifty-eight—also put to death for witchcraft—and Sarah Cloyce, fifty-one, who, though she was accused, escaped death. Nurse's seventy-four-year-old husband, Francis, made wooden trays for a living and was well liked in the community.

According to historians, it is possible that Nurse—an upstanding citizen—was targeted because she and her husband had recently come into a large amount of land and the townspeople were envious of her acquisition. The story behind this coveted land is that in 1678, Francis Nurse had begun renting a large plot of land that included a farmhouse. Because he was hardworking, he would eventually be able to buy the property.

It's also possible that the envy toward the Nurses' resulted from the fact that Mr. Nurse had risen politically in their home-town of Topsfield. There is some clue in historical documents that the city of Topsfield had been in a dispute over its border with Salem Village. The Putnams owned the land on the Salem side. The Putnam family estate was also on this tract of land. If the townspeople were made suspicious and doubtful of Rebecca Nurse, they would be equally suspicious of her husband. To make matters worse, though Rebecca Nurse was strongly affiliated with the church in Salem Town, Francis was outspoken in his dislike of Reverend Samuel Parris and his sermons.

There was also local gossip that Rebecca's mother had been accused of witchcraft years earlier. Although she had never been tried, people believed that witchcraft was passed down from the mother to daughter. Taken together, it is possible that all of these factors contributed to Rebecca Nurse's eventual condemnation. That she had an unblemished reputation was evident in that so many people, who had perhaps kept silent before, came forward to speak for her innocence. The accusers focused only on Rebecca's mother's past, and hence charges were brought against her.

When the accused were not being examined, they waited in prison, and soon enough the prisons began to fill up. On April 19, 1692, while Rebecca Nurse stood chained, Abigail Hobbs, age twenty-two, Giles Corey, age eighty, and Mary Warren, age twenty, were being examined. Three days later, nine more people were examined. Among this group was Rebecca's other sister, Mary Easty. It was not surprising that families and spouses of the accused were arrested, since townspeople believed that witchcraft was contagious. After the examinations, which could last anywhere from three to five days, the accused returned to prison.

Because the jails were usually far away in Boston or Ipswich, a visit to the accused meant leaving the farm untended for a long period of time. If new mothers were in jail, they did not know if

This painting by Tompkins Harrison Matteson is called *Examination of a Witch*. Matteson was born in Sherberne, New York, in 1813. He studied at the American National Academy and was mostly a portrait painter who had an interest in historical situations. The painting is currently housed in the Peabody Essex Museum in Salem, Massachusetts. This painting was commissioned by William D. White of Albany, New York, in 1853. In the painting, a midwife points to an accused woman's naked back, pointing out the "witch's mark." Midwives were often used in examinations to search the bodies of the accused for a mark. The mark could be a freckle or something else completely normal. Since the Puritan dress code was so conservative, it is unreasonable to think that villagers could even determine what an "abnormal" mark would be. They obviously did not have practice seeing one another unclothed.

their babies were getting milk. Author Frances Hill, in *A Delusion of Satan*, writes this about Salem jails: "The jails . . . were places not just of privation but of horror. As the most dangerous inmates, the witches were kept in dungeons. They reeked of unwashed human bodies and excrement. They enclosed as much agony as anywhere human beings have lived. Since they were so close to the banks of the tidal river, they were probably infested with water rats . . . [The prisoners'] limbs were weighted down and their movements restricted by manacles chained to the walls."

One may understand why someone like Sarah Good, who had no money or connections, was accused, but someone like Rebecca Nurse? Nurse was the first of the "unlikely" witches to be accused.

Nurse confessed: "I am clear. For my life now lies in your hands." Nurse's family immediately tried to secure her reprieve. When Governor Phipps granted her one, the accusers once again had fits and the community concluded that this was proof enough that she was guilty.

Nurse was sentenced to death on June 29 and executed on July 19. On the scaffold, she asked God to forgive those who accused her.

It was not until 1711 that Nurse's family was compensated by the government for her wrongful death. Her body had been thrown into a shallow grave on a rocky hill near the execution site. Her family came back late at night and took her body back to their home for a proper burial. In 1885, Nurse's relatives erected a memorial to Rebecca. It wasn't until 1992 that the remains of another accused witch—or wizard, as a male witch was called—George Jacobs Sr., age eighty, were also laid to rest in the Nurse family plot.

1678
REBECCA NURSE HOMESTEAD

IN 1636 FRANCIS WESTON WAS GRANTED THIS LAND UPON WHICH HE LAID OUT A FARM. THIS PROPERTY WAS PURCHASED BY GOVERNOR JOHN ENDICOTT IN 1648, AND IN 1678 FRANCIS AND REBECCA NURSE MOVED HERE AND BUILT A HOUSE. IN MARCH, 1692, 71-YEAR-OLD REBECCA WAS ACCUSED BY CHILDREN OF SALEM VILLAGE OF PRACTICING WITCHCRAFT. NURSE, UPON HEARING OF THE ACCUSATION, EXCLAIMED, "I AM INNOCENT AS THE CHILD UNBORN, BUT SURELY WHAT SIN HATH GOD FOUND OUT IN ME UNREPENTED OF THAT HE SHOULD LAY SUCH AN AFFLICTION UPON ME IN MY OLD AGE?" DESPITE THE AID OF HER RELATIVES AND FRIENDS, NURSE WAS TRIED, FOUND GUILTY, AND HANGED ON JUNE 19, 1692, AND HER BODY WAS SECRETLY BROUGHT BACK TO THE HOMESTEAD FOR BURIAL.
ON APRIL 19, 1775, REBECCA'S GREAT GRANDSON, FRANCIS NURSE, MARCHED FROM HERE TO THE LEXINGTON ALARM, WHICH BEGAN THE AMERICAN REVOLUTION.

DANVERS HISTORICAL COMMISSION, 1977

The Rebecca Nurse Homestead in Danvers, Massachusetts, includes twenty-seven acres of fields, pasture, and woods. This property, cared for by the Homestead Preservation Society, is owned by the Danvers Alarm List Company, Inc. Today, the house includes three restored rooms with period furnishings from the seventeenth and eighteenth centuries. A short distance away on the grounds is a reproduction of the 1672 Salem Village meetinghouse. The meetinghouse was usually where the witches were "examined" by magistrates. This property has been used in film and video documentaries such as Alistair Cooke's *America* (1972), *Three Sovereigns for Sarah* (1985), and *Young Goodman Brown* (1993). Though the plaque states that Nurse died on June 19, she actually died on July 19, 1692.

Nurse's hanging seemed to increase a sense of skepticism among the townspeople. Although more and more people were being accused, the atmosphere in Salem was filled with doom: Neighbors watched neighbors sit in jail while their homes fell into decay and disrepair.

There was a lot of bad feeling surrounding Nurse's death. Widespread skepticism resulted in a backlash against Reverend Samuel Parris. The anti-Parris group would see their heyday. As the trials wore on, Parris continued to preach his stern brand of Puritanism, constantly voicing the vital need to wash away sin. Two years after the trials had run their course, in 1694, Parris was an unpopular individual in Salem. According to *A Delusion of Satan*, Parris said, "Everybody points at me, and speaks of me as by far the most afflicted minister in all New England." Parris finally admitted that he might have been a bit wrong in playing a part in the trials. Regardless of his seeming change of heart, his apology was not accepted. His enemies, those who did not take communion at his church—the elderly Samuel Nurse, Peter Cloyce, John Tarbell, and Thomas Wilkins—were determined to remove him from the parish.

On November 26, 1694, in a statement that he read out in the meetinghouse, Parris admitted that he had spoken in an unadvised manner. It was not until September 1697 that Parris left Salem Village. Salem Village's new anti-Parris committee paid him seventy-nine pounds, nine shillings, and in return, Parris would give up the deed to the parsonage. Then he and his family left for Stowe, Massachusetts. His wife, Elizabeth, died in July 1696. Parris died in 1720 with many debts but enough assets to cover them.

CHAPTER 3

Before Samuel Parris was ousted from Salem, hundreds more were accused of witchcraft. The rich and powerful started to be accused, too. The afflicted girls accused the most influential people in the community. Events spiraled out of control. The girls overstepped their bounds when they "cried out on" Mrs. Margaret Thatcher, the mother-in-law of the magistrate Jonathan Corwin.

In 1692, Judge Corwin was fifty-one years old. His family was one of the most prominent in Salem. The afflicted

JUDGES AND ACCUSERS

girls also accused two sons of former governor Simon Bradstreet and the wife of Reverend John Hale. Eventually, in October, the girls accused Lady Phipps, the wife of Sir William Phipps, their appointed governor from England who had set up the court in the first place. However, none of these society figures were arrested.

The Salem judges were unrelenting in their persecution of individuals. Judge Corwin ignored pleas and letters to end the trials, and Judge Hathorne continued the practice of using the words of the accused against them by bullying them and manipulating their statements.

Judge Hathorne was an extremely religious man. Because of his beliefs in the supernatural, he took accusations of witchcraft very seriously. Hathorne was known for acting more like a prosecutor

This house, known as the witch house, was built in the early 1670s. It is located at the intersection of Essex and North Streets in present-day Danvers, Massachusetts, and was the home of magistrate Jonathan Corwin. When he was twenty-four years old, Corwin purchased the home from Nathaniel Davenport. Although this house is known locally as the witch house, no person ever accused of witchcraft either lived or was imprisoned there. This is the only structure still standing with direct ties to the Salem witch trials. In 1944, the house was nearly destroyed when the city wanted to widen North and Essex Streets. Concerned citizens got together to save the historic home, and the organization called Historic Salem Incorporated was born. Demolition was prevented. Author Enders Robinson describes Corwin in *The Devil Discovered: Salem Witchcraft*: "Corwin's father had settled in Salem in 1638. He had accumulated a fortune, serving in the upper levels of the colony's government. Through fortuitous marriages, the Corwins were allied with the most notable families of Massachusetts. When he was thirty-five, Jonathan Corwin married thirty-one-year-old Elizabeth (Sheafe) Gibbs, a widow who had inherited a great fortune." Corwin is buried near his house, in the Broad Street Cemetery.

Charles Osgood (1809–1891) painted this portrait of author Nathaniel Hawthorne in 1840. Osgood was a portrait painter from Sunham, Massachusetts. This painting hangs in the Peabody Essex Museum in Salem, Massachusetts. Historians believe that it was painted while Hawthorne was engaged to Sophia Peabody and that the picture was a present from Hawthorne to his mother and sisters in Salem. Hawthorne is the author of several great works of literature: *The Scarlet Letter* (1850), *The House of the Seven Gables* (1851), and *Twice Told Tales*—two books of tales with the same title—(1837 and 1842). He was born in Salem in 1804 and is the city's most famous native son. Hawthorne's great-grandfather was the infamous judge Johnathan Hathorne. The author intentionally added the letter *w* to his last name to distance himself from the witch trials and his uncompassionate blood relative.

than an impartial judge. Hathorne died, unrepentant, on May 10, 1717. Author Frances Hill notes in *A Delusion of Satan*: "Hathorne's only comeuppance has been an extremely unflattering character portrayal as Judge Pyncheon in Nathaniel Hawthorne's *The House of the Seven Gables*. Alas, the novel was written a hundred years after Hathorne's death so he never saw himself vividly pictured as a cruel, rigid tyrant. Perhaps sometimes in the small hours he sweated with fear at the possibility that he had caused twenty innocent people to die."

The film *The Crucible*, directed by Nicholas Hytner in 1996, is based on the famous play by Arthur Miller. In the play, the Salem judges—Hathorne and Corwin—are depicted as evil. Miller's drama is still popular today. In March 2002, *The Crucible* opened on Broadway in New York City's Virginia Theater.

According to historians, the young "afflicted" girls may have been very skilled liars who were responsible for many deaths. However, it's also possible that they believed in their own afflictions.

In Increase Mather's "Memorable Providences Relating to Witchcraft and Possessions: A Faithful Account," he made note of one afflicted girl: "In November following, her tongue for many hours together was drawn like a semicircle up to the roof of her mouth, not to be removed, though some tried with their fingers to do it. Six men were scarce able to hold her in some of her fits."

Some judges and ministers wrote down accounts of what they saw and would then use these diary entries as evidence in court. Some other writings that were used to prosecute Bridget Bishop were Sir Matthew Hale's "Trial of Witches" (1662) and Richard Bernard's "Guide to Jurymen" (1627). In addition to reading what acts of evil witches could be guilty of (including appearing bare-breasted or pinpricking someone), there were also judges' "tests."

One such test concerned the Lord's Prayer: If it could be recited without making a mistake, the person was definitely not a witch. (It was thought that Satan would not allow his followers to recite the prayer correctly.) Another sign of being a witch was a witness's testimony of the accused having supernatural strength.

This woodcut engraving of a trial scene during the events in Salem dates from 1692. The artist is unknown. A woodcut engraving is made by incising lines into a piece of soft wood, inking the wood, and printing the image onto a piece of paper. The image is located at the Library of Congress. A lot of art and writing from the seventeenth century did not survive because of cold winters and poor storage facilities. In this woodcut, an older woman stands pleading before the judge while a young girl is "afflicted" on the floor and flails about.

If a poppet—a small doll made of rags and hogs' bristles—was discovered, this was considered hard evidence against the accused (even though there was never any proof that poppets were used to perform dark deeds).

Ann Putnam Jr. accused sixty-two people by the time the witch-hunt was over, and any remaining people in jail were let go in May 1693. Perhaps she really believed at the time that someone or something from the dark New England woods was torturing her. Years later, both of her parents died, leaving her to raise her nine brothers and sisters on her own. Ann, however, did something that none of the other girls in the "circle" did. She publicly acknowledged her role in the witch trials. In 1706, she stood before the church as her pastor read her apology. It read:

> I desire to be humbled before God for that sad and humbling providence that befell my father's family in the year 1692. That I, then being in my childhood, should by such a providence of God, be made an instrument for the accusing of several persons of a grievous crime, whereby their lives were taken away from them, whom now I have just grounds and good reason to believe they were innocent persons; and that it was a great delusion of Satan that deceived me in that sad time, whereby I justly fear that I have been instrumental, with others, though ignorantly and unwilling to bring upon my self and this land the guilt of innocent blood.

Elizabeth Booth, Sarah Churchill, and Mary Walcott—other girls who accused innocent people of being witches—eventually moved out of Salem and married. No one knows what became of seventeen-year-old Elizabeth Hubbard or twenty-year-old Mary Warren. Historian Sir Matthew Hale believes that Abigail Williams went insane.

CHAPTER 4

OTHER MEN OF CONSCIENCE

Throughout the Salem witch trials, it was not just women who were targeted with accusations. Even men who were educated and well respected were brought before the magistrates in Salem. For example, George Burroughs, who was once a pastor in Salem Village, and who had a long-standing rift with the Putnams, was brought to trial.

Before Burroughs lived in the Salem parsonage in 1681, he lived with John Putnam Sr. and Putnam's wife for nine months. Through diary accounts, historians have pieced together that there had been tensions in the Putnam house and, ultimately, Burroughs moved into the parsonage in

This is the arrest warrant for George Burroughs. It is housed at the Massachusetts Historical Society in Boston. Burroughs had graduated from Harvard and was known for his physical strength as well as his intellect. It is possible that his worldliness was a threat to the Putnams. He also had traveled extensively. On April 30, field marshal John Partridge took a shocked George Burroughs from his dinner table in Wells, Maine. Partridge delivered Burroughs to the Salem magistrates on May 4. In questioning Burroughs, judges discovered he did not take Communion and he admitted there were toads in his new home. According to the judges, toads were instruments of the devil. For a complete transcript and a contemporary English translation of the warrant, see pages 53–54.

To Jn⁰ Partredg ffild Marshal

You are Required in their Maj⁴ⁱˢ names to apprehend
the body of m~ George Burroughs at present preacher at
Wells in the provence of Maine, & convay him with all speed
to Salem before the Magestrates there, to be Examened,
he being suspected for a confederacy with the devil in
opresing of sundry about Salem as they relate. I haveing
Received perticuler Order from the Governu & Councill of
their Maj⁴ⁱˢ Colony of the Massathusets, for the same, you
may not faile here in, Dated in portsmouth in the
provenc of Hamshire, Aprill. 30ᵗʰ 1692.

Elisha Hutchinson Maj

By virtue of this warrant, I Apprehended S George
Burroughs and have Brought him to Salem and
Delivered him to the Authority there this fourth
day of May 1692   John Partridge, feild

marshall of the Province
of now hanshir and maine.

Sr. Proc. V. 32.

This painting of the trial of George Jacobs, by T. H. Matteson (1855), is currently housed at the Peabody Essex Museum. It was given to the museum by Charles and R. W. Ropes in 1859. Jacobs was born in England in 1617. When he could not properly recite the Lord's Prayer, he was found guilty of witchcraft. He was outspoken, cranky, and easily enraged. The Puritan community did not think very highly of Jacobs's outbursts. All of these shortcomings could indicate a possible reason for his having been targeted for the trials. He was condemned for practicing witchcraft the first week in August 1692. Jacobs is reported in Frances Hill's *A Delusion of Satan* as having said, "Well burn or hang me. I'll stand in the truth of Christ."

1681. By 1683, his salary payments had stopped. It is possible that John Putnam Sr. rallied supporters to drive Burroughs away. Because he was not getting paid, Burroughs left the parsonage, and the congregation was without a minister. Then, the town threatened to sue Burroughs, who had fled to the town of Casco, Maine. Eventually, he returned to settle his affairs. Putnam wanted to arrest Burroughs, but because Burroughs had made other friends in the town, six villagers came to his defense and he ended up receiving the salary that Putnam had withheld from him. Burroughs then happily returned to Casco.

Nine years later, Burroughs would be taken out of his new home in Wells, Maine, and accused of witchcraft. Twenty-two-year-old Abigail Hobbs and eighteen-year-old Mercy Lewis testified that Burroughs was not only a wizard but also the leader of all the witches. When Burroughs was thrown in prison, thirty-two people signed a petition on behalf of his innocence. However, it was of no use. Burroughs was hanged on August 19, 1692. Standing in front of the crowd, waiting to be hanged, he stunned everyone by reciting the Lord's Prayer perfectly and quickly. Some people called out for his pardon, but the judges refused to hear their pleas. Twenty years later, the government gave his children a monetary compensation for their father's wrongful death.

George Jacobs was not as well respected as George Burroughs. Not only did Jacobs attend church infrequently (a definite strike against him), but he was known for his temper and crude language. When he was hanged with George Burroughs on Gallows Hill on August 19, 1962, he protested, "I am falsely accused. I never did it."

Immediately after the execution, the sheriff and his officers went to Jacobs's house and seized everything the family owned, including Jacobs's wife's wedding ring. After Jacobs was hanged, his family secretly buried him on their own land. In 1864, some of his descendants who were still living on the land unearthed his skeleton—possibly while farming or remodeling the buildings. His remains were taken to Salem in 1992 and reburied as part of a ceremony marking the 300th anniversary of the trials.

This portrait is of Judge Samuel Sewall, who lived from 1652 to 1730. The artist of the portrait is unknown. This painting was commissioned sometime around 1700. Sewall was born in Hampshire, England, and settled in the Massachusetts Bay Colony in 1661. In 1671, he graduated from Harvard. Friends with Governor Phipps, he was appointed to the Court of Oyer and Terminer in 1692. Later in his life, Sewall became known as a famous diarist (one who keeps a diary and then publishes it). He constantly wrote in his diary about the "horror" of the "periwigs" that he had to wear during the trials. A periwig is the fake white hair that British magistrates traditionally wore in court and that are still worn today. He graduated from Harvard and wrote a controversial piece called *The Selling of Joseph* (1700), which was one of the first publications against slavery.

A man that perhaps expressed guilt at the hangings of his fellow man, Samuel Sewall was forty years old when he served on the Court of Oyer and Terminer. Before his career in government began, he married into wealth when he and Hannah Hull were wed in 1676. Sewall was the only judge who ever apologized for his role in the Salem trials, though he had a reputation that would have suggested otherwise—he was known for reducing his children to tears by constantly reminding them of death. In January 1697, Sewall surprised everyone: He handed in a paper at the assembly of the (new) General Court in Boston that stated that he wanted "to take the blame and shame of the opening of the late Commission of Oyer and Terminer at Salem." As recorded in Sewall's diary, he asked that God "not visit the sin of him, or any other, upon himself of any of his, nor upon the land." The new government was happy that such shameful events were over. The whole experience was regretted, certainly, but no one wanted to take the blame.

Though Salem was a small isolated city, outside influences began to infiltrate the troubled town. Two of these influences were Increase and Cotton Mather. Although believers in witches and witchcraft, father and son—both of whom were ministers— were eventually in favor of stopping the executions in Massachusetts. Increase eventually wrote a famous piece that questioned the use of spectral evidence. It was called "Cases of Conscience Concerning evil Spirits Personating Men, Witchcrafts, infallible Proofs of Guilt in such as are accused with that Crime," and it was published in 1693. (It was based on a sermon he preached on October 3, 1692.) This famous piece was published near the time that Increase's own wife was named as a witch, but no charges were brought against her.

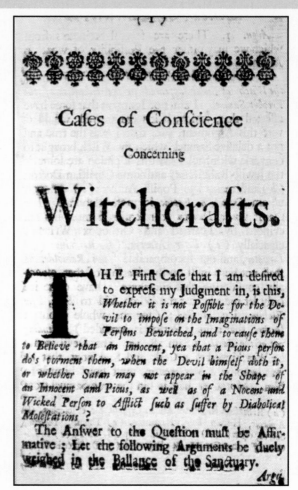

Increase Mather's "Cases of Conscience Concerning evil Spirits Personating Men, Witchcrafts, infallible Proofs of Guilt in such as are accused with that Crime"—the title page and the first page are shown here—is housed at the Massachusetts Historical Society in Boston. This important document caused the course of the Salem trials to be rerouted. This work was first delivered as a sermon to a group of ministers in Cambridge, Massachusetts, on October 3, 1692. It cast serious doubts on the use of spectral evidence. No one knows why these judges took so long to doubt the use of spectral evidence in court. Researchers believe it might have had something to do with the fact that at this time these men were being accused of witchcraft themselves, as were their friends. Mather wrote, "It were better that ten suspected witches should escape, than that one innocent person should be condemned." For a contemporary English translation of the title page and page 1, see page 54. On page 55 is a contemporary English translation of the first page of the preface (not pictured here).

Increase Mather and his son, Cotton, were members of the elite in the colonies. They made names for themselves by documenting several sensational court cases, as well as writing their own philosophies on parenting, morals, and religion. Increase was the son of a wealthy minister who had come to Massachusetts in 1635. (In those days, it was very popular to give children unusual or religious names, such as Reform, More Mercy, Restore, Believe, and Tremble.) Increase, born four years after his father had entered the colony, was given his name, according to Frances Hill in *A Delusion of Satan*, "because of the never-to-be forgotten increase, of every sort, wherewith God had favoured the country."

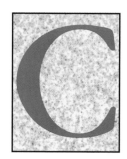# CHAPTER 5

A BRUTAL EXECUTION

It is doubtful that the judges were aware of the horror that people faced in the prisons. Forty-nine people remained in prison when the Court of Oyer and Terminer was terminated on October 29, 1692. Five people had died in the jail: Sarah Osbourne, Roger Toothaker, an unnamed infant of Sarah Good's, Ann Foster, and Lydia Dustin. It is terrible enough to imagine that innocent people were locked up in a wretched jail, but it is even more horrifying to think of the small four-year-old girl, Dorcas Good, who was locked up for eight months. Her mother, Sarah, had already been executed. Dorcas spent her days chained to the wall, able to move only her

This 1692 document, a petition for bail from the accused witches, is currently located in the John Davis Batchelder Autograph Collection at the Library of Congress in Washington, D.C. John D. Batchelder (1872–1958) was a collector of manuscripts and writings that dealt mostly with American history. His collection was transferred from his estate to the Rare Books and Special Collections Division of the Library of Congress in 1961. This petition was most likely penned by the jailer since the accused were usually chained to the wall. The petition illustrates the dismal conditions in the Boston prison. Several of the women were sick, and one had just given birth. In some cases, especially if a pregnant inmate was of low social rank, it was extremely difficult to get food for the child once it was born. For a complete transcript and modern English translation, see pages 55–56.

To the Honourable Governer and Councell and
Generall Assembly now setting at Boston

The humble petition of us whose names are subscribed hereunto
now prisoners at Ipswich humbly sheweth, that some of us have
Lyen in the prison many monthes, and some of us many weekes, who
are charged with witchcraft, and not being consciouse to our selues
of any guilt of that nature lying upon our consciences; our earnest
request is that seing the winter is soe far come on that it can not be
exspected that we should be tryed during this winter season, that we
may be released out of prison for the present upon Bayle to answer what
we are charged with in the Spring. For we are not in this unwilling nor
afrayd to abide the tryall before any Judicature apoynted in convenient
season of any crime of that nature; we hope you will put on the bowells
of compassion soe far as to consider of our suffering conclicion in the present
state we are in, being like to perish with cold in lying longer in prison in
this cold season of the yeare, some of us being aged either about or nere
fourescore some though younger yet being with Child, and one giving suck
to a child not ten weekes old yet, and all of us weake and infirme at the
best, and one fettered with irons this halfe yeare and allmost distroyed
with soe long an Imprisonment. Thus hoping you will grant us a relief
at the present that we be not left to perish in this miserable
condicion we shall alwayss pray &c.

Widow Penny. Widow Vincent. Widow Prince
Goodwife Greene of Hauarell, the wife of Hugh
Roe of Cape Anne, Mehitabel Downing. the wife
of Somaby ay, Goodwife Dicer of Piscataqua
Hanah Bromidge of Hauarell Rachel Hafield
besides thre or foure men

fingers. It is doubtful that any prison warden paid attention to her, thinking she was the devil's servant. When Dorcas was released from the prison, her health had been so severely compromised that her father had to pay a keeper to look after her until she died. She had gone mad.

Some doctors believe that in certain psychological conditions, such as abuse or neglect, a strong desire to hurt or even kill is established. Researchers Carol F. Karlsen, in *A Devil in the Shape of a Woman*, and Frances Hill, in *A Delusion of Satan,* noted that in accusing Dorcas—the child of an outcast who had no one to speak for her—perhaps the afflicted girls were acting out an impulse that comes from having been over-controlled or unloved.

It wasn't enough that people were suffering in prisons and being hanged from trees. Although hanging was the usual punishment for those convicted of practicing witchcraft, other gruesome deaths took place in Salem during the climax of the witch-hunt. On September 19, 1692, Giles Corey, age eighty, was stripped naked, a board was placed upon his chest, and then, while neighbors watched, heavy stones were placed on top of the board. It took two days for him to die. Supposedly, near the end, Corey's tongue came out of his mouth and the sheriff pushed it back inside with his cane. The only words that Corey said were, "More weight, more weight."

At the time of his death, Corey was a prosperous farmer. Ann Putnam Jr., Abigail Williams, and Mercy Lewis accused him of witchcraft. Ann Putnam claimed the specter of Corey visited her April 13, 1692, and asked her to write in the devil's book. Later, she also said that a ghost appeared to her and told her that he had been murdered by Corey.

This is a sketch, circa 1692, of Giles Corey's trial. Corey was the only man to have been pressed to death because he refused to enter a plea. (Throughout the trials, close to 200 people—men and women—were accused.) One theory as to why Corey refused to say whether he was innocent or guilty is that by avoiding a conviction, it became more likely that his farm, which he had just deeded to his two sons-in-law, would not become property of the state after he died. Corey was a devout member of the church, but he had a bit of a tainted past. He was known to quarrel with his wife, Martha, whom he helped send to prison when charges were brought up against her. Corey had been brought to court in 1675 for possibly having caused the death of a manservant by beating him.

(1)

Some Miscellany

OBSERVATIONS

On our present Debates respecting

Witchcrafts, in a *Dialogue*

Between *S.* & *B.*

By *P. E.* and *J. A.* [*Willard, S.*]

Philadelphia, Printed by *William Bradford*, for *Hezekiah Usher*.
1 6 9 2.

Supposed to be written by Mr. Rev'd
Sir, Samuel Willard. See Calef's pamphlet—
More wonders of the invisible world p. 38. Edit. 1

S. I *'Understand that you and many others are greatly dissatisfied at
' the Proceedings among us, in the pursuance of those that have
' been Accused for Witchcraft, and have accordingly sought to
' obstruct them; which I am afraid will prove pernicious to the Land;
' and that for more reasons than one; principally in the hazard of Brea-
' ches and Divisions among us, which tend to some unhappy Change; and
' some-body will be to blame.*

B. Sir, the Peace of a Place is earnestly to be sought, and they that sin-
fully cause Divisions, will be guilty of all the miserable effects of them: but
whether this blame will truly fall upon you or us, is to be considered: there
is an earnest contending for the Truth requisite, and that is not to be
parted with for Peace.

S. 'No doubt every one will justifie himself in his own way; but men
' are not for that Innocent: yea, the most blame-worthy are for the most
' part carried out with the greatest Confidence.

B. True, I could reflect here: but I spare. Only give me leave to

A   tell

This is a debate between the unknown men "S" and "B," printed by William Bradford for Hezekial Usher in 1692. It is housed at the Massachusetts Historical Society in Boston. This dialogue was penned by one person, Reverend Samuel, with "S" representing Salem and "B" representing Boston. It is possible that "B" also represented the voice of Increase Mather. The dialogue discusses what is proper evidence in a witch trial. Many writings on witchcraft were being printed in 1692. For a transcript, see page 56. A contemporary English translation is on page 57.

One theory as to why Corey might have been accused is that he was friends with those who supported Israel Porter, a powerful anti-Putnam member of the community. Corey was examined and then forced to stay in jail with his wife for five months while he awaited trial. When he was brought into the courtroom (a sketch of the court proceedings is shown on page 45), there was a flurry of "evidence" against him. One witness announced that she had seen Corey serving bread and wine at a witch's sacrament. Meanwhile, Corey was quite certain that he would be convicted. Spurred on by the hopelessness of the situation, he did something shocking that had never been done in the history of the colonies—he refused to stand trial. He also pointed out to the judges that no one really escaped the Court of Oyer and Terminer

As planned, the day Corey was taken to court, he refused to speak and stood mute at the bar. The magistrates had to administer "peine forte et dure," which means "strong and hard punishment." Pressing was an old English method of dealing with prisoners who refused to make a plea. It was hoped that the pressing would force the victim to speak. Pressing to death had never been used before that time in New England, and it must have been a thoroughly devastating sight because it was never used again.

CHAPTER 6

THE BEGINNING OF THE END

There were several factors that contributed to the final termination of the Court of Oyer and Terminer in October 1692. Increase Mather's sermon "Cases of Conscience Concerning evil Spirits Personating Men, Witchcrafts, infallible Proofs of Guilt in such as are accused with that Crime" affected how ministers and community members alike thought about spectral evidence. Governor Phipps (shown on the facing page) grew disgusted with the trials when his own wife was named by one of the afflicted girls. What furthered Phipps's desire to take action was a letter dated October 8, 1692, by Thomas Brattle, a wealthy, Harvard-educated merchant and prestigious scientist. In a letter to an unknown correspondent—it began "Dear Rev Sir"—Brattle questioned the prosecution of witches. He did not understand how

This original portrait of Sir William Phipps is housed in the Archives Nationales du Quebec in Quebec City. The artist and the date of the portrait are unknown. Phipps replaced the Court of Oyer and Terminer—made up of his friends William Stoughton, John Richards, Jonathan Corwin, John Hathorne, Nathaniel Saltonstall, Bartholomew Gedney, Peter Sergeant, Samuel Sewall, and Wait Winthrop—with the new Superior Court of Judicature. This court did not allow spectral evidence and condemned only three of fifty-six defendants. Phipps then pardoned those and others who were awaiting execution. In May 1693, Phipps set free any person accused of witchcraft who was still in jail.

The Salem Witch Trials Memorial was dedicated in Salem on August 5, 1992, 300 years after the trials took place. Stone benches placed within the perimeter of the memorial bear the names and execution dates of the victims. There are twenty benches in the memorial, one for each of the victims actively put to death.

spectral evidence could be admitted. He pointed out the errors of the Salem judges in testing the witches, the bullying of the judges, the fact that the afflicted girls became hysterical only in the courtroom, and the fact that they never arrested any accused person related to themselves, such as Jonathan Corwin's mother-in-law. One of Brattle's strongest points was that some people who were accused had never even met the afflicted girls. Brattle then listed reputable men in England who agreed with his point of view and who also condemned the trials.

People were finally growing weary of bloodshed. It did not take long after this letter had been sent for Governor Phipps to write to the Privy Council in London, saying that he had forbidden any more imprisonment relating to witchcraft. On October 29, 1692, Phipps officially dissolved the Court of Oyer and Terminer.

After Samuel Parris was ousted from the parish, the new reverend, Joseph Green, tried to heal the torn community of Salem. Green reshuffled the seating plan of the parish, and the Putnams were seated next to the Nurses. In 1706, Green read the final apology from Ann Putnam Jr., who died, alone, in Salem Village at the age of thirty-seven.

In 1992, 300 years after the trials and executions had occurred, the Salem Witch Trials Memorial, designed by

This is the top of Elizabeth Howe's memorial bench at the Salem Witch Trials Memorial in Salem. Elizabeth Howe's gravestone reads: "If it was the last moment I was to live, God knows I am innocent." Elizabeth Jackson Howe pleaded not guilty to the charge of witchcraft. She was hanged on July 19, 1692.

The proceedings against Sarah Good were particularly cruel since falsehoods were discovered as the trial was going on. One girl cried out that Good's apparition was stabbing her with a knife. Upon examination, a broken knife was found on the girl. Good was hanged on July 19, 1692. A picture of her memorial bench is above.

James Cutler, was unveiled and honored in Salem. It is situated directly across from the site of the old meetinghouse.

More recently, the November 2, 2001, issue of the *New York Times* published an article stating that "more than three centuries after they were accused, tried and hanged as unrepentant witches on Gallows Hill in Salem, Mass., five women have been officially exonerated by the state. The act, approved by Legislature, was signed on Halloween by the acting governor, cheering the descendants of Bridget Bishop, Susannah Martin, Alice Parker, Wilmott Redd, and Margaret Scott." Supposedly, the state had tried to follow through with this procedure in the past. In 1711, all of the accused were exonerated or their relatives were offered retribution. But perhaps because there was still such shame attached to the event, not all of the families came forward to accept this public apology. Then, in 1957, a state resolution cleared the name of one more victim, Ann Pudeator, and "certain other persons." (The 1957 resolution did not list specific names.) It was State Representative Paul E. Tirone who helped push this act through. It stated that the "other persons" should be cleared by name. Mr. Tirone's wife, Sharon, is a descendant of Sarah Wildes, one of the accused women.

According to researchers Paul Boyer and Stephen Nissenbaum in *Salem Possessed: The Social Origins of Witchcraft*, "185 people were accused in Salem, 141 women and forty-four men. Of that number, fourteen women and five men were [hanged], the last group on September 22, 1692." It seemed as if the hysteria would never end.

In 2002, historians are still asking why this hysteria occurred at all. No one knows the exact answer.

PRIMARY SOURCE TRANSCRIPTIONS

Page 21: The examination of Rebecca Nurse at Salem Village

TRANSCRIPTION

24. mar. 1691/2

Mr. Harthorn. What do you say (speaking to one afflicted) have you seen this Woman hurt you?

Yes, she beat me this morning
Abigail. Have you been hurt by this Woman?
Yes
Ann Putman in a grievous fit cryed out that she hurt her.
Goody Nurse, here are two An: Putman the child & Abigail Williams complains of your hurting them What do you say to it
N. I can say before my Eternal father I am innocent, & God will clear my innocency.

You do Know whither you are guilty, & have familiarity with the Devil, & now when you are here present to see such a thing as these testify a black man whispering in your ear, & birds about you what do you say to it
It is all false I am clear

Is it not an unaccountable case that when you are examined these persons are afflicted?
I have got no body to look to but God

Page 35: The arrest warrant for George Burroughs

This arrest warrant, addressed to Field Marshal John Partridge, was issued to arrest George Burroughs. It is dated April 30, 1692. Because Partridge had to travel to Wells, Maine, to acquire Burroughs, Burroughs was not examined by the judges until May 4, 1692.

TRANSCRIPTION

To Jno Partredg field Marshal
You are Required in their Maj'sts names to aprehend the body of mr George Buroughs at present preacher at Wells in the provence of Maine, & Convay him with all Speed to Salem before the Mages-trates there, to be Examened, he being Suspected for a Confederacy with the devil in opressing of Sundry about Salem as they relate. I having Receved perticuler Order from the Govern'r & Council of their Maj'sts Colony of the Masathusets, for the Same, you may not faile herein,

Dated in portsmouth in the provenc of Hamshire. Aprel. 30'th 1692

*Elisha Hutchinson Maj'r

By Virtue of this warrant I Apprehended s'd George Burroughs and have Brought him to Salem and Delievered him to the Authority there this fourth day of May 1692

*John Partridge feild marshall of the
Provence of newhansher and maine

CONTEMPORARY ENGLISH TRANSLATION
To: John Partridge, Field Marshal

In the names of their Majesties, you are required to apprehend Mr. George Burroughs, who is currently the preacher at Wells, in the Province of Maine, and bring him immediately to Salem. He is to appear before the magistrates there to answer questions. He is suspected of having made a pact with the devil to exercise evil power over several people there, as they have testified. I'm issuing this warrant on the orders of the Governor and Council of their Majesties' Colony of Massachusetts. You must carry out the instructions in this warrant. Dated in Portsmouth, in the Province of Hampshire, April 30, 1692.

* Elisha Hutchinson, Major
On the authority of this warrant, I apprehended the said George Burroughs. I have brought him to Salem and delivered him to the authorities there today, May 4, 1692.

*John Partridge, Field Marshal

Page 40: Increase Mather's "Cases of Conscience Concerning evil Spirits, Personating Men, Witchcrafts, infallible Proofs of Guilt in such as are accused with that Crime."

CONTEMPORARY ENGLISH TRANSLATION
Title Page:

Cases of Conscience: Thoughts About Evil Spirits that Impersonate Men, Witchcraft, and the Kind of Proof We Need to Have If We Are to Be Absolutely Certain of the Guilt of People Who Are Accused of Witchcraft.
All of These Things Are Examined According to the Teachings of the Bible, History, Our Own Experience, and the Opinions of Many Well-Educated and Well-Informed Men.

By Increase Mather, President of Harvard College at Cambridge and Teacher at a Church in Boston in New England
Proverbs 22:21—So that you will be able to answer the people who question you with the words of truth.
(LATIN)
Printed in Boston and sold by Benjamin Harris at the London Coffee House. 1693.

Page 1:

Cases of Conscience Concerning Witchcraft.

Here is the first case that I want to discuss: Is it possible for the devil to make bewitched people believe that they are being tormented by a pious person when it is really the devil who is doing it? Is it possible for Satan to disguise himself as a pious person—and not just as an evil person—in order to torture those who are bewitched?

The answer to these questions is yes. Here is my line of reasoning, for you to judge for yourself according to the laws of God.

Following is a contemporary English version of page 1 of the preface (which is four pages) not pictured in text.

Christian Reader.

Civilized people—and religious people even more—so despise the label of "witch" that the name will bring disgrace to anyone who is called that. Because of that, we need to be sure we're not too hasty in accusing someone of witchcraft or too quick to pass judgment on someone who has been accused. The more terrible the crime, the more important it is that we be very careful before publicly accusing someone, especially before God. The wrath of God has set these evil spirits free among us to do horrible things and to cause suffering that is worse than anything ever heard of before this. This has caused thoughtful people to carefully consider how we can detect and defeat the awful plans of the one who is the great enemy of God. All who worship God agree that good can come out of any evil things that are done, no matter how evil those things are. However, even though this is true, the devil has still managed to accomplish part of his plan in quarrels like those that divided the people who followed Moses into the wilderness.

The Bible tells us that there are devils and witches. Our experience confirms that they are common enemies.

Page 43: Petition for Bail from Accused Witches.
This petition is addressed to the governor and general assembly in Boston and was written by several women and men in jail. It is unknown who actually wrote the petition and some names are cut off at the end.

TRANSCRIPTION
To the Honourable Governor and Councell and General Assembly now sitting at Boston:
The humble petition of us whose names are subscribed here unto now prisoners at Ipswich humbly sheweth that some of us have Lyen in the prison many months, and some of us many weekes, who are charged with Witchcraft, and not being consciouse to our selves of any guilt of that nature Lying upon our consciences; our earnest request is that seing the winter is soe far come that we should be tried during this winter season, that we may be released out of prison for the present upon Bayle to answer what we are charged with in the Spring. For we are not in this unwilling nor afrayed to abide the tryall before any Judicature apoynted in convenient season of any crime of that nature; we hope you will put on the bonetts [?] of compassion so far as to consider of our suffering concition in the present state we are in, being likely to perish with cold in lying longer in prison in this cold season of the years, some of us being aged either about or near fourscore some though younger yet being with child, and one giving suck to a child not ten weeks old yet, and all of us weake and infirmed at the best and one fettered with irons this halfe yeare and all most distroyed with soe long an imprisonment. Thus hoping you will grant us a release at the present that we be not left to perish in this miserable concition we shall always pray.
Widow Penny, Widow Vincent, Widow Prince, Goodwife Greene of Havarell, the wife of Hugh Roe of Cape Anne, Mehitabel Downing, the Wife of Timothy Day, Goodwife Dicer of Piscataqua, Hanah Brumidge of Havarell, Rachel Hafield besides three or four men.

CONTEMPORARY ENGLISH TRANSLATION

To the Honorable Governor, Council, and General Assembly now meeting in Boston:

As stated in this humble petition from the Ipswich prisoners whose names are signed below, some of us have been imprisoned for many months, others for many weeks. We are all charged with witchcraft, but none of us knows what we've done to deserve this.

Winter has now progressed so far that it's unlikely that we will be tried before the end of winter. Under these circumstances, we earnestly request that we be released on bail, to return in the spring to stand trial on these charges. We're not afraid to face trial on these charges before any court of justice that would be appointed at a convenient time. We hope you'll find it in your hearts to have pity on us in our present suffering. It is so terribly cold in the prison that we are in danger of dying from the cold. Some of us are almost eighty years old. Some of the younger women are pregnant. One woman gave birth less than ten weeks ago. All of us are weak and ill. One of us has been chained for six months and is almost dead from such a long imprisonment. We hope that you will grant us this temporary release and not leave us to die in such miserable conditions.

As always, we bow humbly before you.

Mrs. Penny, widowed. Mrs. Vincent, widowed. Mrs. Prince, widowed. Mrs Greene of Havarell. The wife of Hugh Roe of Cape Anne. Mehitabel Downing. The wife of Timothy Day. Mrs. Dicer of Piscataqua. Hanah Brumidge of Havarell. Rachel Hafield. Also three or four men.

Page 46: Observations

TRANSCRIPTION

O B S E R V A T I O N S

On our present Debates respecting
Witchcrafts, in a Dialogue

Between S. & B.
By P. E. and J. A.
Philadelphia,
Printed by William Bradford, for Hezekiah Usher. 1692.
This copy used with permission from the Massachusetts Historical Society
© 2000, Rector and Visitors of the University of Virginia
Sir,

S. I understand that you and many others are greatly dissatisfied at the Proceedings among us, in the pursuance of those that have been Accused for Witchcraft, and have accordingly sought to obstruct them; which I am afraid will prove pernicious to the Land; and that for more reasons than one; principally in the hazard of Breaches and Divisions among us, which tend to force unhappy Change; and somebody will be to blame.

B. Sir, the Peace of a Place is earnestly to be sought, and they that sinfully cause Divisions, will be guilty of all the miserable effects of them: but whether this blame will truly fall upon you or us, is to be considered: there is an earnest contending for the Truth requisite, and that is not to be parted with for Peace.

S. No doubt every one will justify himself in his own way; but men are not for that Innocent: yea, the most blameworthy are for the most part carried out with the greatest Confidence.

B. True, I could reflect here: but I spare. Only give me leave to tell you that we have more reasons to plead our integrity by, than possibly you know of or will easily believe.

CONTEMPORARY ENGLISH TRANSLATION
Assorted Observations on Our Current Debates About Witchcraft.
Presented in the Form of a Discussion Between S. and B.
by P. E. and J. A.
Philadelphia, Printed by William Bradford, for Hezekiah Usher.
1692.
Sir,

S. I understand that you and many others are very troubled by the actions taken against those accused of witchcraft and have tried to stop those actions. I'm concerned that your attempts will be harmful to our country, for more than one reason. In particular, I'm concerned that your efforts will cause disagreements and conflicts among us that can only lead to trouble. Somebody will have to take the blame for this.

B. Peace is what we should all want. Anyone who sinfully causes conflicts should be held responsible for all the consequences of those conflicts. However, it remains to be seen whether you will be to blame for these consequences or we will. We also have a responsibility to look for the truth, and we can't avoid that responsibility in the name of peace.

S. People can always find a way to justify their actions. However, just because people can find an excuse for their actions doesn't mean that they're innocent. In fact, the actions that deserve the most criticism are the ones that are usually carried out with the greatest certainty that they are right.

B. That's true. I could go on and talk more about that now, but I won't. Just give me a chance to tell you why we've taken the position that we have. We have more reasons than you might think.

GLOSSARY

affliction The state of being in severe pain, either physical or mental.

apparition A supernatural appearance of a person or thing; a ghost.

arbitrary Depending on individual discretion (as of a judge).

Calvinist A person who follows the Christian teachings and laws of John Calvin, with emphasis on predestination (that one's destiny is preplanned before birth).

charter A document issued by a sovereign state (a self-governing group), outlining the conditions under which a colony is organized and defining its rights.

coven An assembly of witches, especially of the number thirteen.

delude To mislead judgment. A delusion is a false belief.

deviate To differ from the normal.

ergot poisoning Disease caused by a fungus in rye and other cereal grasses. Colonists who became sick with this disease would hallucinate and accuse people based on what they saw.

exonerate To clear from accusation of blame; to unburden.

Gallows Hill The rocky pasture surrounded by water that served as the scene of execution in Salem; also called Witch Hill.

heyday The period of one's greatest success.

immigrant A person who comes to a country to take up permanent residence.

magistrate A local official exercising administrative and often judicial functions.

manacle A shackle for hands; handcuffs.

mania Excitement; disorganization of behavior.

petition A formally drawn request bearing names of those who are asking a person or group in authority a favor.

Pilgrim A seventeenth-century Englishman or Englishwoman who believed in complete separation from the Church of England. Pilgrims settled in the colony of Plymouth.

poppet Earlier word for "puppet"; also an object made from hair and rags with pins sticking out of it, used as evidence of practicing witchcraft.

predestined Something that is decided or put in place prior to birth.

prosecutor A person who brings legal proceedings against another person believing the accused is guilty of a crime.

Puritan A seventeenth-century Englishman or Englishwoman who wanted to "purify" the Church of England by removing all traces of associated Catholic items, such as crosses or vestments. Puritans settled in the Boston area around 1630 and absorbed the colony of Plymouth in 1692.

reprieve A temporary suspension of execution.

specter A visible spirit of terrifying nature.

spectral evidence Evidence accepted by the judges in the Salem courts meant to prove people's claims of specters hurting them.

unrepentant Not showing sorrow or regret for misdeeds.

witch-hunt The searching out and deliberate harassment of those (as political opponents) with unpopular views; a searching out for persecution those accused of witchcraft.

FOR MORE INFORMATION

Due to the changing nature of Internet links, the Rosen Publishing Group, Inc., has developed an online list of Web sites related to the subject of this book. This site is updated regularly. Please use this link to access the list:

http://www.rosenlinks.com/psah/sawt/

FOR FURTHER READING

Currie, Stephen. *The Salem Witch Trials*. San Diego, CA: Kidhaven Press, 2002.

Dolan, Edward F. *The Salem Witch Trials*. New York: Benchmark Books, 2001.

Hill, Frances. *A Delusion of Satan: The Full Story of the Salem Witch Trials*. Cambridge, MA: Da Capo Press, 1997.

Hill, Frances. *The Salem Witch Trials Reader*. Cambridge, MA: Da Capo Press, 2000.

Kallen, Stuart A. *The Salem Witch Trials* (World History Series). San Diego, CA: Lucent Books, 1999.

Mather, Cotton. *On Witchcraft*. New York: Peter Pauper Press, 1950.

Trask, Richard B. *The Devil Hath Been Raised: A Documentary History of the Salem Village Witchcraft Outbreak of March, 1692*. Cambridge, MA: Yeoman Press, 1997.

Woods, Geraldine. *The Salem Witchcraft Trials: A Headline Court Case*. Berkeley Heights, NJ: Enslow Publishers, 2000.

IBLIOGRAPHY

Boyer, Paul, and Stephen Nissenbaum. *Salem Possessed: The Social Origins of Witchcraft*. Cambridge, MA: Harvard University Press, 1974.

Cahill, Robert Ellis. *The Horrors of Salem's Witch Dungeon* (Collectible Classics No. 9). Peabody, MA: Old Salt Box Publishing Co., 1986.

Hill, Frances. *A Delusion of Satan: The Full Story of the Salem Witch Trials*. Cambridge, MA: Da Capo Press, 1997.

Hill, Frances. *The Salem Witch Trials Reader*. Cambridge, MA: Da Capo Press, 2000.

Karlsen, Carol F. *The Devil in the Shape of a Woman: Witchcraft in Colonial New England*. New York: W. & W. Norton and Company, 1988.

Kramer, Heinrich, and James Sprenger. *The Malleus Malificarum*. Mineola, NY: Dover Publications Inc, 1971.

The Mather Papers. Massachusetts Historical Society Collections, 4th Sermon, Vol. 8. Boston, 1912.

New York Times. "Massachusetts Clears 5 From Salem Witch Trials." p. A12, National Report, November 2, 2001.

Robinson, Enders A. *The Devil Discovered: Salem Witchcraft, 1692*. Prospect Heights, IL: Waveland Press, 2001.

Sewall, Samuel. *Diary*. Massachusetts Historical Society Collections, 5th Sermon, Vols. 1–3. Boston, 1918.

Trask, Richard B. *The Devil Hath Been Raised: A Documentary History of the Salem Village Witchcraft Outbreak of March, 1692*. Cambridge, MA: Yeoman Press, 1997.

INDEX

# PRIMARY SOURCE LIST

Page 11: Map of Salem that W. P. Upham created in 1866, which is housed at the Danvers Alarm List Company, Inc., in Danvers, Massachusetts.

Page 14: Contemporary photo of the Sarah Holten house from the Danvers Preservation Commission in Danvers, Massachusetts.

Page 15: Modern-day photo of the Rebecca Nurse Homestead, provided by the Danvers Preservation Commission in Danvers, Massachusetts.

Page 16: Engraving of Judge William Stoughton by R. Babson, circa 1780, housed at the Harvard Law College Art Collection.

Page 18: Sketch of Bridget Bishop by an unknown artist. The date of creation is also unknown.

Page 21: The document "Examination of Rebecca Nurse," written by Reverend Samuel Parris in 1691. This document is now housed at the Peabody Essex Museum in Salem, Massachusetts.

Page 24: Painting by Tompkins Harrison Matteson titled *Examination of a Witch*, which he created in 1853. The painting is housed at the Peabody Essex Museum in Salem, Massachusetts.

Page 26: The contemporary Rebecca Nurse Homestead plaque, which was cared for by the Homestead Preservation Society. It is owned by the Danvers Alarm List Company, Inc., in Danvers, Massachusetts.

Page 29: Contemporary photo by Jim McAllister of the witch house built in the early 1670s and located at the intersection of Essex and North Streets in Danvers, Massachusetts.

Page 30: Portrait of Nathaniel Hawthorne, painted in 1840 by Charles Osgood. The portrait is now housed at the Peabody Essex Museum in Salem, Massachusetts.

Page 32: Woodcut, produced in 1692, of a Salem trial, which is housed at the Library of Congress. The artist is unknown.

Page 35: May 4, 1692, arrest warrant for George Burroughs, which is housed at the Massachusetts Historical Society in Boston, Massachusetts.

Page 36: Painting of the trial of George Jacobs by Tompkins Harrison Matteson in 1855, which is currently housed at the Peabody Essex Museum in Salem, Massachusetts.

Page 38: Portrait of Judge Samuel Sewall, circa 1700, by an unknown artist. Where it is currently housed is also unknown.

Page 40: "Cases of Conscience Concerning evil Spirits Personating Men, Witchcrafts, infallible Proofs of Guilt in such as are accused with that Crime," a sermon circa 1700, which is housed in the Massachusetts Historical Society in Boston, Massachusetts.

Page 43: A petition of bail from the accused witches, which was produced in 1692. It is located at the John Davis Batchelder Autograph Collection at the Library of Congress in Washington, D.C.

Page 45: Sketch, circa 1692, of the Giles Corey trial by an unknown artist. Where it is currently housed is also unknown.

Page 46: Transcript of a debate that was printed by William Bradford in 1692. It is currently housed at the Massachusetts Historical Society in Boston, Massachusetts.

Page 49: Portrait of Sir William Phipps, housed at the Archives Nationales du Quebec in Quebec, Canada. The artist is unknown.

Page 50: Photo of the Salem Witch Trials Memorial, taken in 2001 by Associated Press photographer Lawrence Jackson and housed in the Associated Press photo archive.

Page 51A: Photo taken in 2000 of the Elizabeth Howe memorial bench.

Page 51B: Photo taken in 2000 of the Sarah Good memorial bench.

About the Author

Jenny MacBain resides in New York City and is convinced that her cat, Pixley, is often bewitched.

Photo Credits

Cover, pp. 1, 14, 15, 29, 30 © Corbis; pp. 11, 35, 40 (left and right), 46 © University of Virginia Library; pp. 26, 51 (top and bottom) © Tom W. Stanley; pp. 16, 32, 36, 38, 45 © Hulton/Archive/Getty Images; p. 18 © University of Missouri-Kansas City; p. 21 © *The Colonial Gazette*; p. 24 © Peabody Essex Museum; p. 43 © Library of Congress; p. 49 © Canadian Heritage Gallery; p. 50 © AP/Wide World Photos.

Editor

Annie Sommers

Design

Nelson Sá